Praise for Aldous Remembers

"Paul Hood expertly weaves the comedic, the dramatic, and the bittersweet. Aldous Remembers is one play you won't soon forget."

Lori M. Myers - award-winning writer/playwright

"It's clear that Paul Hood understands how characters should move. He's someone to keep an eye on."

Jayson Ward Williams-Actor/Director

"Wine and memories wrapped within a tale about love; a socially relevant play satiated by currency some will find of high value and sip slowly. In Aldous Remembers, Paul Hood reveals the importance of love and how it pertains to fond memories."

Mary Pat Evans-Educator

"Paul Hood's work is real and honest, touching and inspiring. He has a unique way of looking at relationships and people and creates dialogue that is great for actors."

Dana Kinsey-actress/teacher

Reviews and audience responses to The Itch of Gloria Fitch

"An absurdist play about modern love, "The Itch of Gloria Fitch" is a poignant and sensitive story of a young woman's attempt to discover her place in her own skin"

Ticketfly

"Imaginative!"

"Touching and filled with humor"

"A poetic examination of self-worth and personal discovery"

Praise for My Electric Life

"MY ELECTRIC LIFE is insightful . . . a highly original work, and one that tackles a subject greatly overlooked in current drama."

Broadway World

While "My Electric Life" was inspired by Hood's own Internet habits, most of his other plays that deal with social and mental health issues (along with the absurdities of life) are triggered by the things he sees and hears throughout the city. Plays such as "Other Cat," "Aldous Remembers" (which had its first reading at Midtown Scholar Bookstore) or Hood's longer works—such as "I, Journeyman" and "Brighton's Green Street"—incorporate the rhythm and vibe of urban living.

The Burg

Paul Hood

The Itch of Gloria Fitch

A Play

Paul Hood

Willow Moon Publishing

The characters and events in this book are fictitious. Any similarity to real persons or events is purely coincidental.

Copyright © 2017 by Paul Hood

Published by Willow Moon Publishing
108 Saint Thomas Road
Lancaster, PA 17601
willowmoonpub.com

All rights reserved. No part of this publication may be reproduced or transmitted in any form or by many means except for brief quotations in printed reviews, without the prior permission of the publisher.

Cataloging Data

Hood, Paul (1973-)
The Itch of Gloria Fitch/Paul Hood –1st U.S. Edition
Summary: A play exploring one woman's quest for self-identification.
139 pages ; 14 x 19 cm
ISBN-13: 978-1-948256-07-0

1. American drama-Pennsylvania. 2. American Drama-21st century
    I. The Itch of Gloria Fitch. II. Hood, Paul
    812.54
    Printed in the United States on acid free paper
Typeset: Garamond
Design by Jennie Wiley

The Itch of Gloria Fitch

For Tanaia and Grace; my two reasons.

Paul Hood

Table of Contents

Acknowledgements	11
Why is Hell Hot?	13
Production History	17
Cast of Characters	20
ACT I	23
Scene 1	23
Scene: 2	41
Scene: 3	47
Scene 4	61
ACT 2	70
Scene 1	70
Scene: 2	77
Scene 3	93
Scene 4	107
Scene: 5	117
Scene: 6	121
About the Author	124
Willow Moon Releases	129
Willow Moon Upcoming Releases	135

Paul Hood

Acknowledgements

I would like to thank the Playwright's Alliance of Pennsylvania for their undying support throughout my writing journey along with Artistic Director's Cynthia Charles (Theatre of the Seventh Sister) and Clark and Melissa Nicholson, (Gamut Theatre) my mentor and friend, Marjorie Bicknell, the many talented individuals at Oyster Mill Playhouse, my Pennsylvania family Jennifer, Andy and Marty Rash, my good friends Mary Pat Evans, Tracy Kerchner, my editor, Jennie Wiley and last but not least my family for allowing me to be a writer in the first place, and I cannot forget the theatre communities in Harrisburg and Lancaster, Pennsylvania., without you I'd have a drawer full of plays both unread and unseen.

Paul Hood

Why is Hell Hot?

Someone recently asked me about the value of plays in our modern culture. I considered this for a few minutes and said to myself, 'What is the value of air in our modern culture?' Yes, a far-fetched retort to a simple question, but that's how much I value the need for stories told in dramatic form. The stage is a proverbial breathing apparatus for those of us suffocating, those of us not taking in the truth. It's all about honesty in imaginary circumstances and it seems a good place to fill the air with the aroma of blood, sweat and raw emotion, some of which seems lost today in theaters across the country that struggle to keep the bills paid. Say the word "drama" to a staunch musical theatre enthusiast and you're greeted with a raised eyebrow. Musical theatre makes money, reality or even magical realism does not. It's that simple. Tried and true masterpieces written by great playwrights like the late Edward Albee and

Tennessee Williams are the exceptions, but the little plays "straight plays" that could do not pull the load far enough to satisfy a whole season. How has drama lost its value? What happened to all the eavesdroppers and voyeurs of daily life? Why do audiences no longer care about the stories that move us, the quiet tales of people trying to figure out the confusion we call living?

The valuable thing in all of this are those questions that confuse us; the inquiries that fail to make sense are indeed the catalyst for great stories, stories that we can see and feel. A new breed of playwrights both fearless and unashamed of examining the dysfunctional beings, the addicts, and the taboo are emerging from the depths and corners of our beloved America. Each has a unique story to tell and it is the new way, take it or leave it. Theatre should never be safe or friendly. The stage is not a place for lying. The proscenium should sizzle from start to finish, crackle with the intense heat emitting from desperate souls trying to figure out why hell is hot and why the heck they are stuck in it.

That is the value.

In my play 'The Itch of Gloria Fitch' I take on the task of a young woman trying to work her way through issues of defining herself. Her "Itch"- personified as a male- is convinced it is the love of her life. With this, the adage comes to mind: "If you can't love yourself how can anyone else love you?" and thus it plays throughout, which causes Gloria's skin irritation. I didn't want to approach this story externally as the mind is powerful thing and often the reason we avoid using it at times. I thought it'd be interesting to work from the inside out. I hope you enjoy this examination of a soul not quite highlighted due to its clouded light and the journey ahead to brightness and revelation as much as I enjoyed writing it.

    Paul Hood

    December 2017

Paul Hood

Production History

The Itch of Gloria Fitch received its world premiere during November of 2016. The play was performed at The Capitol Room at Harrisburg's House of Music, Arts and Culture. It was directed by F.L. Henley Jr. and produced by Narcisse Theatre Company.

Production Staff

Writer	Paul Hood
Director	F. L. Henley Jr.
Production Stage Manager	Brianna Dow
Producers	Brianna Dow F. L. Henley Jr.
Sound Design	Brianna Dow
Sound Tech	Dave Nields
Light Design	FrenchFrey Prod.
Poster Design	Mike Fitzgerald

Cast in Order of Appearance

Itch   Clem Onuk

Gloria   Erika Eberly

Doctor Goodall   Ashly Stepp

Dewitt   Robert Campbell

The Itch of Gloria Fitch

Cast of Characters

Gloria Fitch: a young woman, early 20's-30's. Shy but rather cerebral and intelligent.

Dewitt Monday: a young man, early 20's-30's. Sharp and well read, often sarcastic. A graduate of Penn.

Itch: a male the same age range of Gloria. Feisty and confident, a raging sense of self and purpose.

Dr. Goodall: a wise female Physician in her late 30's to 40's.

ACT 1

Paul Hood

ACT I

Scene 1

A doctor's office, rather spare in design, complete with the usual medical items. The lighting is soft, the typical fluorescent. Near center is an examination bed, where Gloria Fitch, (a woman of whatever ethnicity is cast) sits alone, contemplative as she awaits her physician. Gloria is in her early 20's/30's, moderately attractive. Her beauty is hidden under a proverbial veil of insecurity.

Nearby, in a dream-like setting, a man appears. He's clutching a journal in his hands. He is small in stature and dressed in stiff, casual clothing. Near him is a plain chair where he sits and begins to flip through pages until he comes upon one that holds his curiosity. This man is the ITCH, a young-looking male that can be portrayed by a male of any ethnicity. He's just a figment that currently plagues Gloria's life.

Doctor Sylvia Goodall enters. She's attractive but void of intimidation that comes with natural beauty; there is sincerity in her dark, penetrating eyes that are apparent, calmness in her gait. Her hair is of brunette tone, soft curls litter the sides and intermingle-rather suitably-with strands that lay calm and straight. She is dressed in wears not typical to a physician but more like a new-aged therapist. She is in her late 30's to early 40's.

Gloria and Dr. Goodall confer as Itch recites thoughts written within Gloria's journal

ITCH

Gloria wrote this last night, before bed. 'I think I may have some sort of weird skin disease. I'm always itching, even when I lotion my body, which I do quite often because, Dewitt...' (Pauses, slams journal shut)Apparently this *man* has more to offer than I. What is it about him? (Sighs, thinks deeper) Oh, wait...why fret? In theory, I'm much closer to Gloria than that joker. Let's be real: I live beneath the surface of a woman I've loved for many years, and now as the dormancy of my feelings have finally come to a grateful end, she needs to realize it. But what can I do? The plan was to intensify my feelings for her but in a way that wouldn't cause her to see a damn doctor every week. I believe there's something quite broken and hollow about this Dewitt guy and I'm not sure she sees it clearly. Hmm...Oh, I know what I'll do.

I'll just relocate to a potentially embarrassing location and camp out there.

GLORIA

(Hand over heart)

It starts here then moves down toward my stomach, then toward my legs.

DR. GOODALL

The itch?

GLORIA

Yes.

DR. GOODALL

Have you had an allergy test within the last five years?

GLORIA

No.

DR. GOODALL

What type of soap do you use?

GLORIA

An unscented body wash.

DR. GOODALL

How often do you shower?

GLORIA

Probably more than the average woman, maybe too much?

DR. GOODALL

Perhaps you're right.

Short silence accompanied with natural business.

GLORIA

You think its dry skin?

DR. GOODALL

Does it feel more like it's on the surface of your skin or is it internal?

Gloria thinks about this. She scratches her arm, studies it.

GLORIA

Hmm...not sure. Never thought of that.

DR. GOODALL

Skin irritation comes in many forms. For instance: if on the outer layer of the dermis I wouldn't worry, it may just be dry skin, eczema or psoriasis, a number of skin ailments. If internal, I'd consider seeing a specialist that could look further; they may want to do further testing or even a skin biopsy.

GLORIA

I guess it's...internal? It moves around in my body, like a marble does, you know, when it's inside a cloth bag. I'll scratch my chest and it'll move toward my stomach or even my back or arm. Whenever I get to it, it moves to another spot, like it knows and anticipates my wanting to scratch. It drives me crazy!

DR. GOODALL

What time of day is the irritation most severe?

GLORIA

Evening, especially when with I'm with... Dewitt.

Short silence, DR. GOODALL takes note of this.

DR. GOODALL

Family pet?

GLORIA

Uhh, no, my boyfriend.

DR. GOODALL

(Slightly embarrassed)

My apologies. But do you have pets?

GLORIA

I live in an apartment. No pets allowed.

DR. GOODALL

No allergies to certain medications?

GLORIA

Well, come to think of it- can't take any psychotropic drugs. One I used to take made me vomit. Did my previous doctor tell you about the reaction I had?

DR. GOODALL takes a moment, removes a prescription pad and begins to write.

DR. GOODALL

There was nothing in your medical records about an allergy to psychotropic drugs, I apologize. (Pause)Let's start with something simple, to see if we can ease your irritation. I'll prescribe you a corticosteroid, Prednisone. It should offer some relief. In the meantime I'll have you set up an appointment for blood work with the receptionist before you leave.

GLORIA

Was afraid you'd say that.

DR. GOODALL

Wouldn't worry. We'll find out what's causing the irritation.

At left: Itch is reading the journal as he sits on a chair.

ITCH

'I'm sure I'm not allergic to Dewitt. What girl in her right mind would be allergic to the prospect of love?' (Sighs, closes journal) Fuckin' Penn graduate! The Ivy League clone with good symmetry and money; I consider him a bookmark in this read, a place-marker if you will. She's not in love with that starched board of a man. He doesn't spend as much time with her as I do.

The lights transition; up center on a small, but comfortably lived-in studio apartment. It is Gloria's place.

Gloria is standing near her sofa, gently scratching her arm and chest area. Dewitt Monday, a slim, bespectacled man his early 20's with gentle features and the wears of an urban hipster, sits near with a book in hand. Itch remains nearby, observing Gloria and Dewitt's interaction.

DEWITT

(Darts eyes toward Gloria)

Your physician prescribe anything for your skin?

GLORIA

She did; wrote a script for a steroid.

DEWITT

Prednisone?

GLORIA

Yes, a corticosteroid.

Dewitt goes back to reading, and then snaps out of it as he's come upon something.

DEWITT

They say steroids cause weight gain.

Gloria's scratching intensifies.

GLORIA

(Annoyed)

That's your worry?

DEWITT

I'll rephrase: are you worried about side effects?

GLORIA

I want desperately to stop itching like a leper, that's what I want!

DEWITT

Lepers don't itch; Leprosy is a disease that attacks your nerves, makes you feel nothing and leave wounds unnoticed, then your extremities become infected and eventually...you lose them.

GLORIA

(Apathetic)

I suppose.

Dewitt places the book on a small table, relaxes further into the sofa.

DEWITT

Come sit down; thinking about the problem may exacerbate it.

GLORIA

It's actually worse when I sit.

DEWITT

(Casual revelation)

Explains why you never sleep through a night with...me.

Short silence. Gloria ponders.

GLORIA

It's not you.

DEWITT

I know, sorry.

GLORIA

Just a little worried...I went on WEB-MD-

DEWITT

-Why on earth would you do that...?

GLORIA

...And my symptoms clearly point to Hodgkin's Lymphoma-

DEWITT

-With a dual diagnosis of sanity, I hope? (Beat) You honestly think its cancer?

GLORIA

Says itchy skin is a sign of Hodgkin's.

DEWITT

It's allergies.

GLORIA

Why does everyone say that?

DEWITT

Because it's likely you're over-thinking this?

GLORIA

The fact that you're on to something annoys me more than the itch.

DEWITT

(Spreads arms)

Hugs cure everything, and right now you need one. Com'on, I'll squeeze the "itch" out of you.

GLORIA

No.

DEWITT

No?

GLORIA

May be contagious.

Nearby, Itch begins to laugh loudly while reading.

ITCH

(Breaking from laughter)

Smart girl, always has those jabs that graze that clown's broad chin. I'd like to think I'm the reason she's developed a reservoir of sass.

DEWITT

It's not like you have shingles.

GLORIA

Don't old people with compromised immune systems get shingles? (Aside) I think my grandfather had them once...or was it Gonorrhea?

DEWITT

(Attempting humor)

Speaking of compromise...?

GLORIA

(Rolls eyes)

My compromised immune system?

DEWITT

It's *not* cancer. You're fine. Just come have a seat, relax. Maybe it's anxiety. I knew this guy in high school that barfed every time he was anxious. Anxiety can do weird things to your body, like cause itching. It's been proven.

GLORIA

(As if seeing something)

Anxiety.

DEWITT

What, something on your mind?

Gloria saunters toward center, where she takes a seat next to Dewitt as he moves closer to her and begins to gently rub her shoulders.

DEWITT

There, see? All better.

GLORIA

Ever wonder if I inherited this?

DEWITT

No, I highly doubt you have.

GLORIA

Sometimes I need you to humor me.

DEWITT

You want an answer, I know. Sorry I don't have one. I wish I had one. All I know is I want you to feel better.

That's all.

GLORIA

What if I don't? What if this gets worse? It could be something serious!

DEWITT

Oh, you want me to have a remedy rather than be supportive.

GLORIA

No, no, not that-

DEWITT

-I'm here to listen. I wish I had a tangible answer. I hate to see you go through this and not know how to make it better. (Begins closely studying Gloria's back)

GLORIA

I hope this medication works.

DEWITT

(Smirking)

Hey, if it doesn't, just think...at least you'll have curves from taking corticosteroid.

Gloria laughs nervously.

At right, Itch reads...

ITCH

In your heart of hearts and in your soul of souls, I will wear you down, Ms. Fitch. (Pause) Yesterday she wrote: 'Dewitt was so sweet last night. He rubbed my shoulders and endured my endless complaints, which I do believe consumed most of the evening. Although I wonder how long he'll remain patient. (Pauses, gathers a smile) Or maybe he'll leave when I get fat from taking prednisone.' (Stops and moves away from the podium and walks toward center) The deal is-I wouldn't leave. I'll never leave. I don't care if you gain weight. I just need you to scratch, to break your skin, to let me out! Let me love you.

Paul Hood

Scene: 2

Doctor Goodall's office: Gloria is reading-to herself-aloud from a pamphlet while awaiting Dr. Goodall's arrival. Itch, nearby, reads aloud along with Gloria as she recites...

ITCH/GLORIA

'Dermatitis artefacta is defined as the deliberate and conscious production of self-inflicted skin ailments to help satisfy a physical or emotional need...?'

GLORIA

...This is bullshit...

Dr. Goodall arrives.

DR. GOODALL

Good afternoon, Gloria.

GLORIA

So this is it?

DR. GOODALL

Not sure. We can't rule out it may be something you're manifesting.

ITCH

I really have grown fond of this doctor lady.

GLORIA

I mean, this is better than the parasite you mentioned but it also leaves me to believe...

ITCH

...That you love me...

GLORIA

...That I'm such a basket case I may be causing my own symptoms.

DR. GOODALL

You're not a basket case. More people struggle with this than you know.

GLORIA

Can I meet them?

DR. GOODALL

...Umm...Well...

GLORIA

...A physical or emotional need?

DR. GOODALL

You mentioned you itch more during evening.

ITCH

...It's Dewitt...

GLORIA

...Seems that way...

DR. GOODALL

...I have an assignment for you...

GLORIA

..An assignment...?

DR. GOODALL

Assess your environment and the moment your itching intensifies, and then record it.

GLORIA

Write it down?

ITCH

Yes, Gloria, write down when you profess your love for me.

DR. GOODALL

It doesn't have to be detailed.

ITCH

It will be. Trust me.

GLORIA

This'll be interesting.

ITCH

No, it'll be good for you to realize you need me more than you need Dewitt, which is what I've been trying to tell you since you thought about going to that damn diner to get rid of your hangover that morning. I mean, seriously...I was there when you mentally professed your concern about Dewitt's longing for pumpkin spice lattes! I recall your eloquent composition with clarity! You wrote: *what kind of man drinks pumpkin flavored anything?!*

DR. GOODALL

Until your blood work comes in I need you not to worry. Focus on documenting when the irritation starts, that's what's important now.

GLORIA

I'm sure I won't have a problem with that.

Silence as Gloria ponders this.

DR. GOODALL

(Breaking in)

Look, I know this is a scary moment for you but you'll be fine. Just keep seeing me regularly and we'll figure out what's beneath.

GLORIA

Easier said, you know?

DR.GOODALL

I know. Just...trust is key here.

GLORIA

(Not convinced)

Trust.

The lights fade on Dr. Goodall's office and come up on Gloria's apartment.

Scene: 3

Gloria's living room: She stands alone while scratching furiously. Nearby, Dewitt enters and watches her for a while. In his world, Itch is enraptured in his usual voyeurism of Gloria's life.

DEWITT

I can hear you scratching from the other room.

GLORIA

It's getting worse.

DEWITT

You're going to open your skin.

GLORIA

Good, then maybe I can rid myself of whatever it is and replace my skin with something that makes sense.

DEWITT

Something like...?

Silence. Gloria studies her welted arms.

GLORIA

Plastic?

DEWITT

That wouldn't work; you'd have to worry about...heat.

GLORIA

Melting away sounds like a good idea, progress; then I could be reshaped into something healthy, less confused.

Silence as Dewitt goes about natural business before taking a seat.

DEWITT

You need to see a specialist.

GLORIA

(Exhausted)

Not the specialist again.

DEWITT

What is it now?

GLORIA

Dr. Goodall said something about a specialist.

DEWITT

I'm sure she did when she realized the medicine wasn't working.

GLORIA

A grim reaper dressed in a lab coat, that's what a specialist is to me; and with my luck this *"specialist"* will be young and pretty, pretty enough to make me feel more flawed and diseased than I am.

Dewitt shifts his position, as though Gloria's statement has taken a swing at him.

DEWITT

I must be a horrible boyfriend.

GLORIA

You're fine.

DEWITT

Okay, well *"fine"* is how one describes a grade of hair.

GLORIA

I want to assure you...

DEWITT

...You itch more when I'm around! (Short silence) Have you noticed?

Gloria stops scratching and begins nervously rubbing her arm. Itch, hearing this, is quite taken and moves closer to Gloria's world.

GLORIA

I do?

DEWITT

(Solemn)

Guess I never noticed before myself.

GLORIA

(Nervously)

Not true. I itch all the time, Dewitt. I itch at work, I itch on the bus, itch at the movies, the bookstore, and the yoga studio, everywhere!

DEWITT

You've been scratching harder since I came over. (Beat) Or maybe you've gathered a weird fungus from your yoga mat?

GLORIA

Dewitt you're way too smart for horrible attempts at humor.

DEWITT

I'm deflecting. You're right...

Short silence. A revelation looms.

GLORIA

I-

DEWITT

-When I was young my mom used to clean when something bothered her, and she only did it when I was around. I was stupid enough-or maybe too smart for my age-to realize she did it because she was young herself, too young to deal with my painful idiosyncrasies. Cleaning was a useful distraction, I guess.

GLORIA

I like you the way you are.

DEWITT

I'd like to like myself again, like myself as much as you like yourself when you're with me, the way you used to before the itching. But lately-each time I'm around-you're scratching the life away from not just your skin but us too! (A breath) I feel like I'm the cause.

GLORIA

But you're not.

DEWITT

It's too late to tell me anything different.

GLORIA

How long have you felt this way?

ITCH

Tell'em, Gloria!

DEWITT

I dunno.

GLORIA

What are you saying?

DEWITT

Nothing...I think.

GLORIA

Is this why you came over earlier than usual?

DEWITT

That has nothing... (Loses thought)

Short silence

GLORIA

How long?

Gloria begins scratching.

ITCH

(Whispers)

Tell'em you love me.

DEWITT

How long have I what?

GLORIA

Who is she?

Itch begins searching around his space, only to return with the journal in his hand. He flips the pages with vigor until he lands upon a page...

ITCH

(Reading aloud)

'Sometimes I feel like Dewitt may have someone else in the shadows, someone behind my irritation, my pain, which-I feel weak and helpless for thinking-follows him everywhere.'

DEWITT

There's no one else!

GLORIA

I'm struggling to believe you right now!

DEWITT

Please work on that, the 'believing me' thing. I think it's important for our relationship.

GLORIA

Work on being straight with me, being honest. That's important too.

DEWITT

There's no one!

Long silence. Gloria paces.

GLORIA

(Softly)

Sometimes I wish there was.

Strong silence. Dewitt saunters toward the couch, sits.

DEWITT

How unfortunate.

GLORIA

(Regretful)

I'm sorry.

ITCH

Vindication!

DEWITT

I'll assume your declaration is a result of your relentless *irritation*.

ITCH

It's because of me, you worthless germ! She loves me!

Itch refers to the journal.

GLORIA

I didn't mean that.

DEWITT

(Mumbles to himself)

I can hear my mom vacuuming the living room.

GLORIA

Huh?

DEWITT

Nothing.

GLORIA

What does this mean...for us? What is this?

ITCH

It's over; that's what it means. It's the perfect time. Dewitt's barely hanging on.

DEWITT

Maybe we need a break.

GLORIA

(Forlorn)

It's become a job?

DEWITT

I don't know what to do anymore. I feel helpless. I'm supposed to be able to help you, right?

GLORIA

You're leaving me?

DEWITT

No, no. That's not what I mean.

GLORIA

You're wading in that area, that *gray* area.

DEWITT

I don't know...maybe we need time apart?

GLORIA

Time apart?

DEWITT

Guess I was expecting you to really fight with me. This feels too easy, like no effort at all for you to pull away.

(Beat)

GLORIA

All I can think or feel right now is how bad I feel inside and out.

DEWITT

Well then...maybe space is what...we...what we need...

Dewitt fades under light at left. Gloria, saddened by Dewitt's exit, removes her shirt and begins scratching her body with intensity.

Itch moves slightly toward center, closer to Gloria. He reads from the journal gloatingly.

ITCH

Dewitt left last night and I'm not even upset about it. Maybe I expected him to leave. Honestly, I don't blame him. I would've done the same thing. I don't have the patience or strength Dewitt has...or had? I wonder if...'(Itch pulls his eyes away from the journal, begins pacing within his light)

Of course he won't come back! He's never felt for you like I have. He's not a part of you! He's...a...a passing theme, a relic of a man with no capacity for love. I'm sure you see this. I sure do. I'm here for a reason. I'm the suitable, valiant cliché'(laughs) a lovable parasite. Extract me and take me as I am!

Scene 4

A few days later: Dr. Goodall's office.

Dr. Goodall

We've tried everything it seems. I think we should look at alternative treatments.

GLORIA

It's not topical at all, is it?

Dr. Goodall

I'm afraid not. My guess is it may be something you've perhaps created through anxiety.

GLORIA

It's not cancer...but I'm...crazy?

Dr. Goodall

I've ruled out a serious illness, even allergies. Gloria, it's why I had you read about-

GLORIA

(Dismissive)

-Yeah, Dermatitis Artefecta...

Dr. Goodall

Preliminary blood test came back normal. We should refer you to a...psychotherapist.

GLORIA

I'm so screwed up my mind causes me to itch?

Dr. Goodall

Have you had any recent life changes? Any changes in sleep or your diet?

GLORIA

I cut back a little on red meat. Oh, wait...could it be a gluten thing?

Dr. Goodall

Highly doubt that. Look, I know a great therapist. I'll set up an appointment for a visit.

Dr. Goodall begins writing. Gloria looks around the room nervously.

GLORIA

My only life change is a personal one.

Dr. Goodall pulls away from writing. She appears unsure of what to say.

My boyfriend...he couldn't deal with...the 'condition.'

Dr. Goodall

(Genuine)

Sorry to hear that.

GLORIA

It's probably best, right?

Dr. Goodall

You need support during this-emotional support. I'm sure you have plenty of friends, right?

GLORIA

I do. But sorta got caught up with being in... I thought I was in..."Like." (Slight laugh)

Dr. Goodall

It's good you can see the humor in this. Positive thinking does serve its purpose.

GLORIA

I avoided them though, my friends. I was too wrapped up in my relationship.

Dr. Goodall

May I ask why?

Gloria appears surprised by Dr. Goodall's inquiry.

GLORIA

Scared of losing another person I care about.

Dr. Goodall

Fear lies in the soul that cares.

GLORIA

That's...nice; never heard that before. Pretty sure I scratched away anything logical or poetic.

Dr. Goodall

Maybe you were numb to it all. The feel-

GLORIA

-Feeling in a dream I've craved for so long now.

Dr. Goodall

But you do feel and that's good. I'd worry if you didn't, from a medical perspective, I mean.

GLORIA

Maybe I feel *too* much? Maybe the itching is all my feelings trying to push through, rise up, and reach a certain place, a boundary where the sensation is left to dance against the underside of my skin.

Short silence. Dr. Goodall smiles softly.

Dr. Goodall

I'll look into prescribing a topical agent.

GLORIA

Can you remedy my failed love life?

Dr. Goodall

(Softly)

There may be side effects.

GLORIA

The kind I wouldn't mind, I'm sure.

Gloria and Dr. Goodall share a laugh.

Dr. Goodall

We're going to do our best to help you. I want to assure you nothing indicates you have a serious illness. We've explored all possibilities, the physical ones.

GLORIA

The silver lining.

Within the silence the lights fade gently on Dr. Goodall and Gloria. At left, Itch appears under light, dressed in an immaculate suit while holding the journal.

ITCH

'I wish Dr. Goodall was a single man and not a woman. Wait, I shouldn't think this. I should think of Dewitt. Maybe he did love me and I was too oblivious and scratched away all things that mattered. Not sure what I was thinking. I probably wasn't thinking. I was...clawing...' (Itch pulls his eyes away from the journal) It's working. I'll be the first to admit I never thought I'd break the surface. But, in all honesty, the most difficult part awaits me. Yeah, I have to convince her friends and family I'm what's right for her. Now, how can I do this without completely losing her? (Returns to journal) 'Hopefully Dr. Goodall comes back with an answer I want to hear, one I'm ready to face. I don't care what it is; I need to hear something so I can make sense of this. I already miss Dewitt.' (Itch scoffs, stops reading) Hmm...I may have to up the ante...

At center the lights return on Gloria, standing still under the light as she shares the silence with Itch. They gaze contemplatively toward the darkness.

Paul Hood

ACT 2

ACT 2

Scene 1

A few days later: Dewitt sits in a chair, slumped and comfortable and slightly buzzed from Scotch. Flanking the chair is the liquid culprit: a glass poured two-fingers high, a double, sits half filled on a small table.

DEWITT

This is my fault. Another one lost because of something out of my control. (A breath thinks) Or was I in control? Was it I that made her skin crawl? Oh God, I was the itch! I'm diseased, a carrier of some type of skin bug, a parasite? Wait, no, no, I'm doing that. No thinking I have some kind of communicable skin disease because I'll start itching. What I should think-or do-is be a man and call Gloria. I gave up on her too easily. She's probably sitting alone in her apartment-scratching-and thinking I don't love her. (Thinks) Yeah, that's what I'll do. I'll call her! I'll be a man, the man I am...!

Removes cell phone from his pocket; attempts to dial but hesitates.

DEWITT

...Yeah, tomorrow...tomorrow I'll be a man.

Two spotlights illuminate the far left and right of the scene where Gloria and Itch sit contained in their separate yet equal worlds. As though she has just removed herself from a bath, Gloria is wrapped tight in a towel. Itch is doing his usual: reading from Gloria's journal as Gloria writes within it. After a moment of natural business, they ponder...then Itch crosses, breaking the barrier between their worlds.

ITCH

(Reading aloud)

'...Thankful my problem hasn't moved somewhere I'd be embarrassed to explain to friends and family.' (Sighs, pulls away from reading) I've spared you that but...only out of love. I probably would've resorted to hiding somewhere...inconspicuous if you'd stayed with that pretentious, urban clone you were so infatuated with. Have you shelved the memory of him that fast? I've seemed to have lost his name, what was it...?

DEWITT

(Sighs)

...Dewitt...

ITCH

'...I miss how he shaved my legs while I lay in the bathtub...' Oh, shit, not that memory. I hated that event; him being that close to you drove me crazy. But I couldn't make you scratch then. It was too soon. But I do remember the awful mistake, the razor too close, the pressure just a little too much as he removed the first layer of skin from your shin bone and, how the blood leaked into the bath water and turned the soapy soup of your intertwined bodies a gentle shade of pink...

GLORIA

(As though out of a trance)

I miss him.

ITCH

No, you don't. You're lonely; you miss the *idea* of him.

GLORIA

But...I know calling him would make me look weak.

ITCH

Yes, I agree: weak. You don't want to look weak. I know how strong you are...inside.

GLORIA

But I haven't itched as much lately since we split.

ITCH

There's a reason for that.

GLORIA

I wonder if it was him. Was I allergic to the man of my dreams or allergic to the possibility that I'd lose him one day? Did my body know this?

ITCH

No, I knew. Do I have to explain it again?

GLORIA

Oh what do I know; hell the multitude of doctors I've

seen don't have answers either.

ITCH

But you do know! You're blinded, you'll see in time. Keep scratching and you'll remove me and we will be together when it is right, and right is coming soon. I'm nearing the extraction point, I can feel it! I'm just having a little trouble reaching it. (Sighs) Was hoping I'd reach it by now...something's getting in the way... At first I thought it was more than Dewitt, but I'm afraid it is indeed only him. Could it be something inside of you other than me and Dewitt's nagging presence?

GLORIA

Could there be something growing inside of me?

ITCH

Could there be something...?

A sharp pause; Gloria and Itch sit in silence. Soon, Itch violently flips through the journal.

ITCH

I don't see anything. Gloria, com'on! You have to write what you know. Did the doctor tell you something you're not revealing to me? Why haven't I seen this...what is it?

Gloria removes herself from her seat and slowly exits.

ITCH

(Revelatory)

I'm not physical? (Pauses, runs his hands over his person, frantically) Gloria, come back! You have to finish writing!

Silence.

Itch, rather pitiful, flips pages in the journal. He does this within the quiet for a few before the lights fade to black.

Paul Hood

Scene: 2

A week later: Dewitt is sitting at a table at center, his phone in hand. Contemplative, he looks over the dial pad.

Gloria enters, dressed in perhaps her best dress. It is flowing and light, a flattering texture that highlights her svelte yet, aching body.

GLORIA

(Dewitt darts his eyes toward his watch)

I'm late.

Awkward silence.

DEWITT

Wait, wait, you're wha-?

GLORIA

Late. I'm always late, you know that.

DEWITT

Oh, you mean late as in...time?

GLORIA

Uh, yeah. (BEAT) What'd you think I meant?

DEWITT

Thought you were about to drastically change both of our lives.

GLORIA

Oh, you thought?-

DEWITT

Thought you were going to tell me you were-

GLORIA

-We hardly have sex, Dewitt.

DEWITT

I know but-

GLORIA

-Was just saying I was late getting here...

DEWITT

You're not. I'm early, I think.

GLORIA

At least we're both here, right?

DEWITT

Yeah, we are. We are.

GLORIA

How are you?

DEWITT

You beat me to that question. I'm fine. It matters more how you are.

They sit and stare at each other lovingly, as though mentally reshaping moments they once shared.

GLORIA

(Ashamed)

I'm stalling.

DEWITT

No, please do. I like...when you...stall.

GLORIA

You never told me that before.

DEWITT

Secretly, I liked a lot of things about you I never mentioned.

GLORIA

Thought my small talk annoyed you.

DEWITT

...In my world, people talk too big sometimes. It's exhausting, trying to climb up the hills created from elitists' rhetoric.

GLORIA

Interesting.

Gloria shamefully scratches her head.

GLORIA

I'm sorry.

DEWITT

It's ok.

GLORIA

The itch has moved to a more natural place-except when I scratch in public people still give me weird looks.

They share a genuine laugh.

DEWITT

So, it's better?

GLORIA

Well, that's why I asked you to meet me.

DEWITT

Oh.

GLORIA

It's going to hopefully be better after I get...after I get...therapy

DEWITT

Therapy?

At left Itch fumes as he reads the journal.

ITCH

'I never thought anything would manifest itself inside of me unless it was Dewitt's child.' (Stops reading) I knew it. The fear in your mind and heart, no wonder I couldn't get through! That's what's keeping me from getting to the one place I need to be--

GLORIA

--It's psychosomatic.

DEWITT

Psychosomatic? Wait, wait...

GLORIA

...It's what's causing me to itch. Don't you see? It wasn't you!

Dewitt's at a loss for words. He searches...

ITCH

Tell'em, tell'em where it is and watch him run away like a scared child. He doesn't have the guts to see you through anything!

GLORIA

I wasn't expecting you to take it-

DEWITT

Huh, take what... that I couldn't be there?

GLORIA

You shouldn't worry.

DEWITT

I'll worry! You can't keep me from doing something so natural to me. I...I love you!

Short silence.

ITCH

Oh, please, no, not now!

GLORIA

You what? Now, now you say it?! Dammit, Dewitt.
(Gloria begins to well with emotion)

DEWITT

I'm...hey, don't...

ITCH

It's fine, fine. I know you do but you have...fucked up timing!

DEWITT

...I...

GLORIA

It's all in my head!

Dewitt takes this in.

DEWITT

How...well, if this was all in your head I wonder what was ever in...your heart?

ITCH

Yeah, you idiot. I was in her...that's why I can't get to her. You've cluttered her brain with falsities. It's why neither of us can break through!

GLORIA

It's not as bad as it sounds.

DEWITT

What can I do? Just tell me. I want to be there for you.

GLORIA

I needed you weeks ago, Dewitt!

DEWITT

I know but I'm here now. I'm standing here, right now, telling you I love you and I want to be there for you and make this as easy and comfortable as I know how. That's all I can do!

GLORIA

Then, why now? Why now when it's bad and not when it was good, like before I started scratching my skin off and trying to figure out what was beneath the woman I am.

DEWITT

I know what's beneath you-what's in your mind-I know you love sunsets during summer, the rain at night and how it sounds like distant applause when it hits the leaves on that old oak tree outside your bedroom window. I know these things because I know you and I've failed to tell you I knew and loved all of this while you were irritated and confused, and I'm sorry for that. I want to make it up to you.

ITCH

No, he doesn't. Don't fall for it, Gloria!

Gloria starts to gently scratch her arm.

DEWITT

I'm sorry. I've upset you. I should go.

GLORIA

No, not yet.

DEWITT

You're scratching again. I made it come back.

GLORIA

Strange, I *haven't scratched* in days. The days you were gone.

ITCH

It's me!

DEWITT

When's your first session?

GLORIA

Next week.

Short silence, Dewitt turns in his seat and stares out into the distance.

DEWITT

I want to be there. I want to be there for you.

GLORIA

Dewitt, you don't have--

DEWITT

--I won't take no for an answer...

ITCH

...How unfortunate...

GLORIA

...Are you sure?

DEWITT

Right now, in this moment...more sure than ever.

ITCH

I have to get to the surface before this clown.

GLORIA

Don't know what to say.

DEWITT

Just say you want me there.

GLORIA

I was ready to come here and let you off the hook and you surprise me, telling me you *love* me. I'm so confused.

DEWITT

But I'm not confused. Not anymore.

ITCH

...Shit...this asshole's smoother than I thought.

GLORIA

You're not?

DEWITT

Let me back in.

ITCH

There's not enough room...

GLORIA

Didn't think you'd want to go through this.

DEWITT

I'll go through anything with you, Gloria.

GLORIA

Say it again.

DEWITT

I will absolutely go through anything with you.

GLORIA

One more time...

Gloria and Dewitt walk slowly toward each other and embrace.

The lights fade on their intertwined bodies and remain on Itch, who is now beside himself and tearing through the journal with fury.

Paul Hood

Scene 3

Weeks later: Itch is in his world, with his head inside the journal, reading. He appears rather disheveled and still, slightly perturbed. Around him are pages from the journal, which lay strewn about all over, some crumpled, and others lay flat.

ITCH

Fucking hate new age therapists.

Nearby sits Gloria, dressed in comfortable jeans, a shirt and flats. She's at the end of a conversation on her cell phone. In her ear are a set of blue tooth ear buds.

GLORIA

That's right...think positive. I'll do that.

Gloria disconnects and goes about natural business. Itch begins to read aloud from the journal...

ITCH

'I was irritated for so long this feels like a new birth of

sorts. No part of me feels real now and I love every minute of it. I can function. I didn't know I wasn't functioning; I was merely on some kind of auto-control, a woman of perfunctory actions not living a full and happy life. Is this what I've been...missing?'

Dewitt enters, smiling softly as he watches Gloria in her element. He does this with admiration as Gloria does not notice his presence.

ITCH

Oh, great. Look who it is.

Dewitt clears his throat, rather loudly...

GLORIA

(Turning)

Oh, hey...how long...?

DEWITT

...Long enough to realize something I never noticed.

GLORIA

And that is?

DEWITT

Your ass looks great in those jeans.

GLORIA

And where is Dewitt and why is there a clone of him in my apartment?

DEWITT

Never told you that before?

ITCH

You haven't.

GLORIA

Maybe you just *thought* it.

DEWITT

That's...almost terrible.

GLORIA

I like this new thing we have.

ITCH

There's a *thing* now. That's the problem. I have to get to my destination and break out. I've been blocked by new mental inhabitants and Gloria's forgetting about me. This is some most unwanted shit!

DEWITT

I like this new thing too. I made a promise to myself that I wouldn't hold back how I feel anymore.

GLORIA

I like it. Keep it coming?

DEWITT

(Jokingly)

Don't get needy.

GLORIA

Know what I need right now...?

DEWITT

Is it what I think?

GLORIA

Wanna *try a new form of...*?

DEWITT

...An impromptu session?

ITCH

Oh, com'on, don't do it now...!

Dewitt and Gloria approach each other, a passionate embrace ensues, kissing, caressing...

GLORIA

(Pulls away, begins gently scratching her chest)

Wait, wait, the doctor said...I shouldn't get too involved...physically, I mean. Not until I...

DEWITT

...How long did she suggest? And it is a suggestion, right?

GLORIA

When was the last time we had sex?

Awkward silence, Dewitt tugs at his disheveled shirt.

DEWITT

Can't remember...right now I'm pretty sure all of my blood has rush toward my *other* brain.

GLORIA

What if...What if we find out this is something else that...needs work?

DEWITT

(As though he's thought of this before)

Oh, great...way to lower the sails...

ITCH

(Deadpan)

This is the most awkward conversation I've witnessed between these two.

GLORIA

Maybe we should wait. Just to be safe.

DEWITT

Maybe I should move to that small town in Lancaster County?

GLORIA

At least you still have your sense of humor and improved the timing of it.

DEWITT

Hey, Conan O'Brien went to Harvard, remember?

GLORIA

Speaking of Conan, maybe we should watch TV. instead.

DEWITT

I need a cold shower because right now I'm having a surge of testosterone *like* Conan the Barbarian.

GLORIA

Who the hell is Conan the Barbarian?

Silence, stares.

GLORIA

Oh, right, television.

DEWITT

Cold shower.

They quickly exit in opposite directions.

ITCH

I almost had to watch- and listen- to her making love to that stiff, Ivy League android. (the thought makes Itch shiver) Okay, devise a new plan of assault on the senses.

What other route can I take to get to the love of my life? I've tried everything, now I'm blocked, left to remain in a form of dormancy. I'll figure this out...just need a few ideas to spring forth.

Itch begins looking around his space, picking up the strewn papers lying about. He comes across one of the sheets, and studies it intensely. He does this for a full minute. It is intensely quiet.

ITCH

(A realization)

She does love me.

Next day. Gloria is writing in her journal. Nearby Dewitt is putting his clothes on. Itch is nearby, reading the journal.

DEWITT

I hate to confess this but I often wonder what you're writing in that journal.

GLORIA

Just thoughts; random things.

DEWITT

About...?

GLORIA

Life.

DEWITT

So, I'm...in your journal?

GLORIA

I can't reveal any part of this.

DEWITT

(Disappointed)

Oh.

GLORIA

It's a journal, Dewitt. That'd be like me asking to see and read everything you think. Could you imagine how awful it'd be to see and read the thoughts of someone close to you?

DEWITT

I guess.

GLORIA

I wouldn't want to know certain things you think about me and I sure wouldn't want you to know things I think.

DEWITT

Oh, really?

GLORIA

Yes, really. It's the mystery that makes us love each other. The things unknown, not seen. The surprises; if I knew everything you thought there'd be no need to explore the depths of you. It's why I hate when people say, 'I'm an open book.' Sometimes we want the book to open when we choose to open it, not when the pages are revealed beforehand.

Short silence.

DEWITT

I've never heard you talk like this. You seem...

GLORIA

...The discoveries, the finds, the little things...

More pondering.

DEWITT

I guess you're right.

Dewitt finishes dressing. Gloria continues writing.

ITCH

Just when you think someone wants you out of their life they surprise you; Gloria, always full of *little surprises*.

The lights return on Gloria and Dewitt.

DEWITT

I'm going to head out, have a few things to do.

GLORIA

Are you ok?

DEWITT

I'm fine. Why?

Gloria stands, approaches Dewitt and hugs him. He reciprocates the embrace.

GLORIA

You're worried. I can feel it.

DEWITT

What is there to worry about?

GLORIA

I feel like a new person. Is that scary for you?

DEWITT

It makes me happy.

GLORIA

I hope so. I want you to be happy.

The lights fade to black on Gloria and Dewitt.

Scene 4

Itch has made progress. He appears to be much closer to Gloria. Gloria is at her writing space as Itch stands center, an ominous glow of light above his figure as he reads Gloria's confessional.

ITCH

'Dewitt came over a few days ago and as soon as he walked in I looked at him and knew it was not the same for us. I had that punch-in-the-gut feeling. It was awful, but also a huge relief. I admit I was only in love with the idea of being loved by someone else when I knew I should have love myself all along. And, sadly, I think Dewitt felt the same when he confessed to me how he loved me. I think he was enamored with the old me, the sick me, the one possibly nearing the end of her life, a person he could love only because her existence was something not promised. I knew something was wrong when he came in that day. I just had that awful rush...'

Itch disappears under a black out. From right Dewitt enters. It is few weeks earlier.

DEWITT

Am I interrupting your writing?

GLORIA

No, I was just finishing.

DEWITT

It's cold outside.

GLORIA

It is?

DEWITT

Yeah, guess I didn't dress for the weather.

GLORIA

(Aside)

We're talking about weather.

DEWITT

Oh no, we are. Am I that guy?

GLORIA

What guy?

DEWITT

The guy that's not interesting has nothing to say anymore-so he talks about mundane things to fill in space.

GLORIA

No, why would you...?

DEWITT

...I don't have an answer.

Short pause

GLORIA

Something wrong?

Dewitt crosses the room, sits on the couch and stares.

GLORIA

Well say some--

DEWITT

--That's it; I don't have anything to say.

GLORIA

What?

DEWITT

What I mean is...I thought I was there, you know? I thought I was going to lose you. I kept imagining us having an awful breakup, the kind with loose ends and questions, then having none of the ends tightened and you dying and me regretting how I hurt you. But you see, you're all better now and you're strong and it's beautiful and I see you're fine, just fine without me and I feel like I have nothing more to offer.

GLORIA

But you offer more than you know, Dewitt.

DEWITT

The things a friend can offer, maybe. And hell, that's not a bad thing, is it?

Silence, Gloria begins pacing.

GLORIA

(Halts, stares at front door)

This evening with us-I rehearsed it all in my mind-and it hasn't gone the way I imagined.

DEWITT

In that case I feel like an extra in a scene that was cut.

GLORIA

(Revelation)

One I've always allowed you to direct.

At left, from the darkness. Itch steps into a sliver of majestic light.

ITCH

Bullshit, Gloria! You're in control here. It's your life, your need to discover the love I feel for you. Don't look at him. He's your weakness. Be strong...

GLORIA

Funny.

Gloria begins to scratch, almost perfunctorily.

DEWITT

You're itching again?

GLORIA

Huh? Oh, no, this is a natural...

DEWITT

...How long have you been itching?

GLORIA

...It's not like the itching I had before; this...this...actually feels...nice.

DEWITT

How's itching feel nice?

GLORIA

Can't explain it; it's like something trying to get out of me-and when I scratch it feels like I'm helping to extract it-and it excites me to know there's something within me I've yet to see-or find or even feel within myself.

Uncomfortable silence.

DEWITT

Exactly what it looked like to me; it was like you were trying to scratch so hard you wanted to become fragments, shavings of a woman unrecognizable to me.

GLORIA

I don't *recognize* myself. I haven't, in years! Somewhere between high school and college...and a shitty state job-I lost the girl who was happy and confident, free and adventurous, lovable! Not just lovable to others but lovable to herself.

DEWITT

I loved you. Still do. I love you enough to know your discovery is worth exploring, and it's worth exploring on your own.

Silence as pondering commences.

GLORIA

I guess it is.

Gloria sits next to Dewitt on the couch.

DEWITT

I loved you when you needed it. I feel good knowing you don't need to be loved anymore, not by me, not by anyone. Not until you're ready.

More silence.

GLORIA

Where does this leave us?

DEWITT

Without scars.

The lights dim. Itch moves closer.

ITCH

Didn't see that coming; in her journal she said she missed the itch, the feeling, the way she scratched as though she wanted to unearth a new woman; that she hadn't realized it then but that's what she needed to do, and not having to scratch any longer made her feel as though she had given up on finding what was beneath. (Breath) We were looking for each other.

Itch exits left, disappearing into the darkness.

Lights return on Dewitt and Gloria.

DEWITT

We did something good, for us.

GLORIA

We did.

DEWITT

I don't think I would've learned empathy.

GLORIA

I don't think I would've learned...about me...and the things I want to see from myself.

DEWITT

I still love you. I always have.

GLORIA

I know.

Dewitt stands to leave, he walks toward the door. Gloria follows and as Dewitt turns toward Gloria's direction to say one last goodbye, she greets him with a hug. It is a long, silent moment.

Scene: 5

A few days later: Dr. Goodall's office.

Dr. Goodall

Your skin has healed nicely.

GLORIA

Thank you. I was afraid I'd scar.

Dr. Goodall

A natural worry; you're lucky, your skin is one of the most resilient I've come across.

GLORIA

(Accepting this)

Yeah, yeah, it is...

Dr. Goodall

Well, let's get you on your way--

GLORIA

--I want to thank you.

Dr. Goodall

Just doing my--

GLORIA

--No, you treated me like a person. I just want you to know that.

Dr. Goodall

You're human, Gloria. I'm a Physician. It's my duty, my oath.

Dr. Goodall heads for the door. Then, as though she's had a small revelation, she stops near the door and turns back toward Gloria.

Dr. Goodall

Truthfully, I think it was you that saved yourself. I was just there to provide...let's just call it...a manual of sorts. You built the new you.

Dr. Goodall exits, fades into the darkness at right. All is quiet for a moment as Gloria looks around the sterile confines of Dr. Goodall's office, as though she'll never see it again.

GLORIA

(Gently rubbing her arm)

Thanks for saving me.

Paul Hood

Scene: 6

It is a few weeks later, Gloria's apartment. It is quiet, early afternoon when her front door opens. Gloria, standing in her doorway, looks reborn, beautiful and fresh.

Itch appears under a new, much brighter light, a new journal in hand. He begins to recite. While Itch reads, Gloria enters her apartment and goes about natural business.

ITCH

Gloria wrote this a few days ago: 'I've unearthed a new, fantastic thing. I'm sure this has been some kind of primitive, painful rebirth. In the end though, I'm happy I've gone through this suffering, the loss, the change...the wondering. What I have underneath the old Gloria is a woman restored, renovated, clean with possibilities, optimism under new flesh I scratched away from uncertainty.'

Itch appears satisfied.

Itch walks off into the darkness, a confident stride. Gloria is now relaxed and comfortable on her couch. Before her, on the coffee table, sits her journal; she gently removes it from the table and begins to write, journaling quietly for a little until alerted by a knock at her door.

As Gloria gazes in the direction of her door contemplatively, there's another knock. Then with all the confidence she's missed most of her adult life, she remains seated and continues to write with passion.

End of play

The Itch of Gloria Fitch

About the Author

Paul Hood is a Playwright/Director from Harrisburg, PA, and a graduate of Harrisburg Arts Magnet School. His plays have received productions throughout the Tri-State area as well as Central Pennsylvania. His most recent works produced: My Electric Life produced as a workshop production by Theatre of the Seventh Sister and performed at the Steinman Theatre. The Imposter's Snow Cone Machine produced by Playwrights Alliance of Pennsylvania and performed at Hershey Area Playhouse as well as The Itch of Gloria Fitch, which had its world premiere at Harrisburg's House of Music, Arts and Culture's Capitol Room and was produced by Narcisse Theatre Company.

Paul Hood is also a writer and voice actor for Oyster Mill Playhouse' Radio Theatre. His most recent works for the stage were as director for Susan Lori-Parks' Pulitzer Prize winning play, Topdog/Underdog produced by Narcisse Theatre Company and Superior Donuts written by Tracy Letts produced by Oyster Mill Playhouse. He lives in Harrisburg, Pennsylvania.

Previously Published Plays: Aldous Remembers: published by Off The Wall Plays, London.
http://www.offthewallplays.com

… The Itch of Gloria Fitch

From Off the Wall Plays, Aldous Remembers by Paul Hood

Aldous Bentley has a problem: he is prone to dangerous sleep walking and forgetfulness. His memory often eludes him; he can't remember his wedding day, or precious moments he's accumulated in his life. Now, after one year of marriage to his beloved wife Wanda, he often fails to remember anything that involves their time together.

One night during a small gathering at the home of their longtime friend's Vance and Lisa Shante' Aldous confesses to Vance in the kitchen that because of his inability to remember significant moments with Wanda, he feels he may not be in love with her, and that she is the wrong woman.

Meanwhile in the living room Wanda confides in Lisa that she too is not sure she married the right man, and that his fleeting memory and odd sleep walking has smothered the fiery passion she once had for Aldous. With lost memories from Aldous and growing frustration from Wanda, will the Bentley's love survive this early test in their marriage?

Lovers of fine wine, the Shante's and Bentley's soon discover the complications involved in matrimony. Only time and the partaking of fine libations bought from their meeting place of Ithaca, New York, a place for which both couples share fond memories, will tell in this touching drama as each come upon revelations in their marriages.

Aldous remembers, a drama layered with humor and honesty examines the connection of love and memories, and how we deal with the potential realities of losing people we cherish in our lives and the moments we spend with them.

Willow Moon Publishing

Started at the kitchen table by two friends, Willow Moon Publishing works to provide access to quality books that all too often are overlooked by the "Big 5". Our goal is to help authors who tell engaging, dynamic, and compelling stories get their work into the hands of readers. Willow Moon considers it their mission to bring the works of women and minority authors into the forefront of the publishing world.

We provide print, ebook, and audio book publishing services. We also offer marketing services for your manuscript at reasonable prices.

Email us at wileystapler@gmail.com for more information about getting your book published and/or marketed.

www.willowmoonpub.com

Find us on Facebook @willowmoonpublishing

Willow Moon Releases

**Samuel Stanley Scotty Snight
by Alison Broderick
Illustrated by Mina
Anguelova**

Meet Samuel Stanley Scotty Snight, a redheaded, freckle-faced, chubby second grader who loves to eat! From potatoes and steak to cookies and cake, he is passionate about mealtime.

Unfortunately, good dental hygiene does not interest Samuel as much as satisfying his hunger.

Samuel Stanley Scotty Snight will not brush his teeth at night, and consequences soon follow.

Age Range: 2 - 10 years

Paperback: 42 pages

1st edition December 6, 2017

Language: English

ISBN-10: 1948256037

ISBN-13: 978-1948256032

Product Dimensions: 8.5 x 0.1 x 11 inches

Deadtime Stories by Kathryn Viers

Deadtime stories is a collection of short stories, published posthumously by the author Katherine Viers, ranging from surreal to sci-fi and from fantastic back to the intensely personal and moving.

Written over the span of a decade, Viers gives the reader a gripping connection to her believable characters, pulling us in with the raw and vulnerable humanity of their lives.

She uses a revolutionary pared down technique with dialogue that amps up the intensity of the tales.

Paperback: 138 pages

1st edition November 18, 2017

Language: English

ISBN-10: 1948256045

ISBN-13: 978-1948256049

Product Dimensions: 5.1 x 0.3 x 7.8 inches

SH Levan edited by Jodi Stapler

For the history buffs, these home recipes and news clippings collected by S.H. Levan in the early 1900's in Lancaster County, Pennsylvania give a real life picture into the everyday life of the simple, hardworking people of Victorian Pennsylvania. It's an excellent opportunity to get a peek into what the life is like for the Amish people today.

Paperback: 34 pages

1st edition May 22, 2017

Language: English

ISBN-10: 1546852417

ISBN-13: 978-1546852414

Product Dimensions: 6 x 0.1 x 9 inches

Little Dragon Flies in the Sun
by Jennie Wiley

An exciting second printing is upcoming in 2018 with a new illustrator.

A little dragon, who lives in a dark cave, faces her fear and sets out into the daylight to find others like herself. A story of loving yourself and chasing your dreams.

Grade Level: 1 - 2

Paperback: 32 pages

1st edition (May 18, 2017)

Language: English

ISBN-10: 1546795294

ISBN-13: 978-1546795292

Product Dimensions: 8.5 x 0.1 x 11 inches

Willow Moon's Audiobooks
Find our selection of classic stories retold as well as an original story about Miss Pepperoni, a rescue pup's tale of finding a home, on Audible.

Willow Moon Upcoming Releases

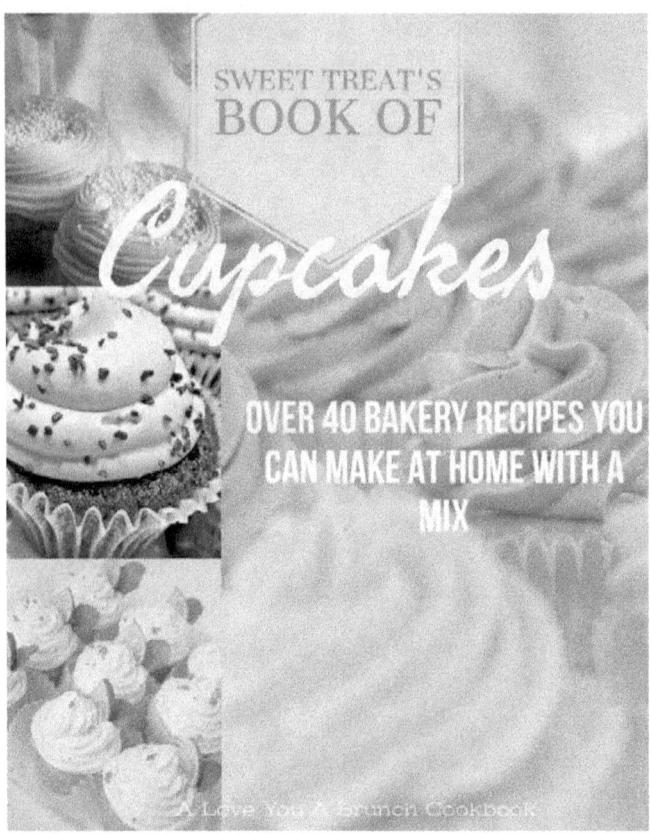

A cookbook from the Sweet Treats Owner and Love you a Brunch podcaster, Jodi Stapler, filled with decadent and delicious cupcake recipes.

Make a Wish on a Fish
by Jennie Wiley and illustrated by Mina Anguelova

A whimsical story about finding magic in the world around you by simply applying your imagination

Six Chicks Go to Yoga
by Jennie Wiley and illustrated by Nina Makolkina

This upcoming 2018 release teaches yoga to children through the charming story of six little chicks.

The Itch of Gloria Fitch

www.ingramcontent.com/pod-product-compliance
Lightning Source LLC
Chambersburg PA
CBHW071737080526
44588CB00013B/2064